BASIC DESIGN
For Beginners

YOUNES ZEINALI

CONTENTS

INTRODUCTION

SCOPE AND OBJECTIVES OF THE BASIC DESIGN COURSE

OBJECTIVES AND COMPETENCIES TARGETED FOR STUDENTS IN THE BASIC DESIGN COURSE

COMPOSITION

DESIGN ELEMENTS

1. POINT-LINE
2. TONE (VALUE), LIGHT - SHADOW - VALUE
3. TEXTURE
4. COLOR
5. STAIN
6. SHAPE - FORM - DIMENSION
7. SPACE - FULLNESS
8. DIRECTION

BASIC DESIGN PRINCIPLES

1. REPETITION
2. BALANCE AND RHYTHM
3. HARMONY
4. CONTRAST
5. UNITY
6. INTERVAL (SPACING)
7. DOMINANCE - EMPHASIS
8. PROPORTION - SCALE

THREE-DIMENSIONAL DESIGNS

CONCLUSION

PREFACE

Design is the artful expression that emerges from the creative exploration of ideas formed in our minds. It is a process of transformation, where existing concepts or elements are reimagined and reshaped into something entirely new. In every facet of our lives, we are constantly surrounded by design; whether consciously or subconsciously, our choices are often guided by the effectiveness of these designs. Nature itself is an ever-present source of inspiration, offering countless examples of artistic expression that enrich our senses and elevate our appreciation for beauty. This natural influence inherently shapes our standards, preferences, and expectations in design.

While design is rooted deeply in artistic principles, it plays a pivotal role in shaping our everyday experiences. We find ourselves drawn to those designs that feel the most intuitive, resonating with our natural sense of balance and harmony. The formal journey to integrate design into educational frameworks began with the Bauhaus movement, which established design as a structured and disciplined field of study. This approach has evolved into an essential aspect of modern life, influencing fields ranging from architecture and industrial design to product development and visual communication.

Today, as the role of design in society becomes increasingly prominent, courses focused on foundational design principles have become indispensable components of art and design education. Primary Design Education teaches the fundamental elements and principles that underlie all creative work, offering a versatile foundation that benefits learners from various disciplines. These courses broaden perspectives, equipping aspiring designers with the essential techniques, materials, and skills to navigate the creative process.

The objective of Basic Design Education—and, in turn, this book—is to unlock the creative potential of emerging designers. It aims to empower them by providing practical tools, diverse methodologies, and a framework for original thinking. By fostering an environment of exploration and encouraging diversity in thought, this book seeks to inspire students to push the boundaries of conventional design and embark on innovative, creative journeys.

This book is designed for educators who guide foundational design courses and learners beginning their creative journeys. It serves as a comprehensive guide, supporting exploration, experimentation, and the development of a unique design voice.

Younes Zeinali
Ankara, 2024

01
INTRODUCTION

BASIC DESIGN

The "**Basic Design**" course, universally recognized by this name, is a foundational component in the first-year curriculum for disciplines such as graphic design, fine arts, and architecture. Typically extending over two semesters, it is one of the most pivotal and rigorous courses in a designer's educational path, seamlessly integrating theoretical concepts with hands-on practice. The primary aim of this course is to develop essential skills, including observation, perception, creative thinking, and problem-solving, through the exploration and application of various materials and techniques.

At its core, Basic Design endeavors to enhance students' visual cognition by focusing on the systematic utilization of visual elements and principles. By presenting diverse methodologies, the course motivates students to experiment, innovate, and craft varied compositions employing various materials. The ultimate objective is to nurture artistic creativity, enabling learners to freely explore their abilities while extending the limits of their creative potential.

This visual exemplifies a geometric composition that reflects the fundamental elements of basic design. The balanced use of shapes, colors, and spaces underscores the importance of visual thinking and creative composition skills.

THE FOUNDATIONS OF BASIC DESIGN

The term "Basic Design" is derived from the Greek word "emulsion," meaning "foundation," combined with the English concept of "design," which implies the act of creating or planning. This course is structured to be more than just an introduction to design; it serves as a framework for expressing creative thoughts through a systematic approach. Here, design transcends the mere production of visually appealing forms, aiming instead to convey deeper meanings through thoughtfully crafted compositions.

This foundational course equips students to transform abstract ideas into tangible visual expressions. Learners are encouraged to translate their observations into compelling design solutions by enhancing their sensory awareness and cultivating imaginative skills. The result is a harmonious integration of aesthetics and meaning, allowing students to express their inner world through creative visual narratives.

AND EVOLUTION OF BASIC DESIGN

THE HISTORICAL CONTEXT

Integrating design into formal education traces back to the Bauhaus movement, which revolutionized art instruction by adopting a multidisciplinary approach. Established in 1919 by architect Walter Gropius in Weimar, Germany, the Bauhaus School sought to unify art, craft, and technology to enhance living conditions through modern design.

Students experimented with industrial materials at the Bauhaus, moving beyond traditional artistic limitations. The curriculum combined fine arts and design education elements, balancing theoretical knowledge and practical application.

This approach encouraged creative freedom alongside technical precision, preparing students for the evolving design landscape.

Despite its closure in 1933 due to political pressures, Bauhaus's influence persisted globally. Former educators and students migrated, particularly to the United States, where they continued teaching and shaping the future of design education. The Bauhaus's legacy endures in contemporary design principles, emphasizing functionality, simplicity, and the harmonious integration of form and purpose.

THE ROLE OF GESTALT THEORY IN DESIGN

Gestalt theory, a cornerstone of Bauhaus philosophy, emphasizes holistic problem-solving by asserting that the perception of a whole surpasses the mere sum of its parts. This perspective enables students to grasp the interrelations among elements within a composition, fostering a comprehensive understanding of design. Integrating Gestalt principles into the curriculum encouraged an experimental design approach, prompting students to move beyond isolated components and focus on the unity of form.

At the Bauhaus Gestalt psychology's theories on perceptual organization and aesthetic perception, she played a pivotal role in design education. Wassily Kandinsky's "Point and Line to Plane" explorations align with Gestalt psychologists' research, delving into how essential visual elements interact to form cohesive compositions.

Additionally, designers like György Kepes actively incorporated Gestalt theories into design education, particularly during his tenure at the New Bauhaus in Chicago between 1937 and 1943. Fusing these theoretical foundations with practical experience elevated Basic Design beyond a purely technical subject. This methodology balanced creative exploration with meticulous analysis, enriching students' design perspectives. Consequently, Basic Design evolved into a discipline of enduring theoretical significance, influencing generations of designers.

DESIGN EDUCATION IN THE POST-WAR ERA

After World War II, American art institutions adopted and expanded upon the principles established by the Bauhaus School. Initially known as "Vorkurs" in Germany, the course became widely recognized as "Basic Design" in the United States, solidifying its role in art education. This period emphasized simplified designs, functionality, and the use of economically viable materials, reflecting the era's social and technological changes.

Technological advancements, notably the invention of photography, transformed the art world by introducing new visual possibilities. Photography, followed by cinema and television, blurred the lines between art and technology, creating new forms of creative expression that continue to shape design today. As industries and technologies evolved, design education adapted by continuously emphasizing functionality and user-centered design.

MODERN APPLICATIONS OF BASIC DESIGN

The Basic Design course remains a fundamental component of design education, guiding students in translating their observations and creative impulses into practical design solutions. It provides a comprehensive foundation for understanding the interplay between form, function, and meaning. By exploring historical contexts and contemporary techniques, the course equips aspiring designers with the skills necessary to navigate the complexities of modern design challenges.

In today's era, where the boundaries between art, technology, and industry continue to blur, the principles taught in Basic Design are more relevant than ever. EncouThe Basic Design course is an essential pillar of design education, empowering students to transform their observations and creative ideas into practical design solutions. It lays a strong foundation for understanding the relationship between form, function, and meaning. By delving into historical contexts alongside contemporary techniques, the course equips aspiring designers with the skills necessary to confront the diverse challenges of modern design.

In a world where the distinctions between art, technology, and industry are increasingly intertwined, the principles taught in Basic Design have never been more critical. This course inspires students to question norms, explore possibilities, and innovate boldly, enabling them to craft solutions that captivate the eye and meet real-world needs with practicality and elegance. Raging students to question, explore, and innovate, this course prepares them to develop solutions that seamlessly combine aesthetic appeal with functional effectiveness, addressing real-world needs.

THE IMPACT OF BASIC DESIGN EDUCATION

The Basic Design course pivotally equips students with the skills to transform their observations and creative impulses into practical design solutions. It provides a solid foundation for understanding the intricate relationship between form, function, and meaning. By delving into historical contexts and contemporary techniques, this course prepares aspiring designers to navigate the multifaceted challenges of modern design adeptly.

In today's rapidly evolving landscape, where the lines between art, technology, and industry are increasingly blurred, the principles imparted in Basic Design are more pertinent than ever. The course encourages students to question conventions, explore innovative ideas, and develop solutions that harmoniously blend aesthetic appeal with functional effectiveness, addressing real-world needs.

SCOPE AND OBJECTIVES OF THE BASIC DESIGN COURSE

The "Basic Design" course is an immersive exploration into the foundational elements and principles forming visual communication's backbone. Integrating theoretical knowledge with practical studio exercises aims to cultivate the creative and technical skills needed to advance to more complex design projects. Its purpose extends beyond igniting visual creativity; it seeks to nurture critical thinking and technical proficiency, offering a comprehensive toolkit for emerging designers.

This book establishes a universal design language, bridging the diverse educational methodologies across institutions worldwide. While design education may vary in cultural and institutional contexts, the fundamental elements and principles remain universally consistent. By synthesizing these foundational concepts into a cohesive and structured framework, this book provides a flexible yet thorough guide that can be applied in any setting.

Structured into a systematic plan of 16 core elements and principles, the book equips learners with a robust and adaptable skill set, empowering them to tackle modern design's complexities confidently. It aims to arm aspiring and experienced designers with the tools to transform theoretical insights into tangible, creative outputs, fostering a profound and enduring understanding of design fundamentals.

Moreover, this book guides readers in developing problem-solving skills through a creative and practical approach, enabling them to effectively meet the demands of contemporary design. It highlights the critical interplay between art, technology, and functionality, demonstrating how these realms can harmoniously converge in modern design practices. Beyond teaching design principles, it inspires readers to craft unique visual identities and explore sustainable design, encouraging the intelligent use of resources in creative projects.

DESIGN
ELEMENTS OF

- **POINT-LINE** — *1*
- **TONE - LIGHT - SHADOW - VALUE** — *2*
- **TEXTURE** — *3*
- **COLOR** — *4*
- **STAIN** — *5*
- **FORM-SHAPE-DIMENSION** — *6*
- **SPACE-FULLNESS** — *7*
- **DIRECTION** — *8*

DESIGN
PRINCIPLES OF

REPETITION — 1

BALANCE-RHYTHM — 2

HARMONY — 3

CONTRAST — 4

UNITY, INTEGRITY, HARMONY — 5

SPACING — 6

DOMINANCE-HIERARCHY — 7

SCALE-PROPORTION — 8

ESSENTIAL CONCEPTS IN BASIC DESIGN

The Basic Design course is fundamental in cultivating essential skills for aspiring designers. It emphasizes the development of creative thinking, enabling students to effectively utilize elements such as color, shape, and form and to conceptualize in two and three dimensions. Students learn to craft a unique design language by integrating observation with thought and employing plastic elements to organize cohesive compositions.
A vital aspect of the course is addressing artistic challenges, fostering an understanding of expressive languages, and nurturing individual expressive styles. Students analyze the interplay between form and space, enhancing their ability to think three-dimensionally and execute structural practices proficiently. Moreover, the curriculum encourages awareness of contemporary innovations and technological advancements, guiding students to incorporate these techniques into their design projects.

EXPECTED OUTCOMES OF BASIC DESIGN

- The ability to think freely and creatively while integrating contradictions is essential.

- Recognizing external stimuli during the creative process enhances problem-solving skills.

- We are developing patience as we master techniques and materials.

- I am gaining the courage to experiment again, even after failures, while adapting to the rapid pace of technology to enhance my work.

Due to the rapid advancement of technology, the Basic Design course has integrated computer programs into its curriculum. This incorporation has made it easier for educators to convey the course content, allowing for diverse and innovative applications. This topic has become increasingly prominent in recent years, and computer-supported design programs have expanded the range of teaching methods and techniques.

However, traditional hands-on design exercises still play a crucial role alongside this digital integration. Including three-dimensional and even two-dimensional design tasks enriches the program, enhancing students' understanding of design fundamentals. Additionally, using digital platforms, students can apply their ideas within a virtual environment, exploring new possibilities for expression and experimentation.

Illustration and painting activities have found their place in the Basic Design course, encouraging students to develop their creativity within digital mediums. The rapid pace of the digital world enables students to bring their ideas to life quickly, often within short timeframes, thereby expanding their creative horizons beyond traditional limitations.

Furthermore, the digital environment allows students to continuously engage with new visual trends, keeping them up with the ever-evolving design landscape. This integration into the curriculum promotes a broader vision, helping students observe and participate actively in the digital art world.

Educators must possess the skills to adapt to these technological advancements. Generally, the instructors of this course specialize in this field, but over time, other professionals who are experts in different areas of art education can also contribute to the program. This flexibility allows for a rich exchange of experience and techniques, enhancing the teaching of design fundamentals.

In summary, the Basic Design course aims to teach design principles and adapt to the technological changes of the modern age. The goal is to provide students with a solid foundation in traditional and digital design techniques, enabling them to excel in a rapidly changing creative industry.

03

OBJECTIVES AND COMPETENCIES TARGETED FOR STUDENTS IN THE BASIC DESIGN COURSE

The primary goal of Basic Design education is to enhance the student's perspectives, cognitive abilities, sensory perception, and thought processes. It aims to develop these skills and make them applicable in different fields. Students trained in basic design acquire foundational knowledge to use effectively in their respective domains. This way, they do not just become consumers of pre-existing information but also creators of new knowledge.

While only some people who study Basic Design are expected to become artists, the aim is to develop an aesthetic sensibility and visual perception. At the end of this educational journey, students are expected to create an aesthetic personality, enhancing their visual sensitivity, which in turn helps them interpret, visualize, and transfer their ideas into creative outputs. This course ensures that individuals gain a strong foundation in the principles of art, enabling them to understand and apply design elements at the highest level. It aims to prepare students for the next stage in their creative education journey. Completing this course equips students to tackle more advanced art and design projects, allowing them to explore materials and techniques confidently.

04
COMPOSITION

Composition is the art of thoughtfully organizing the visual elements that form the essence of a design. It is the strategic process of arranging parts or components on a visual plane to create harmony, balance, and clarity. In essence, composition transforms individual elements into a cohesive whole, making the viewer's experience visually pleasing and meaningful.

Composition is about guiding the viewer's eye through the artwork, establishing a visual flow that enhances the message or emotional impact. It acts as the invisible structure within a piece, creating pathways that naturally draw the eye. Whether you consciously notice it or not, a strong composition often captivates your attention when looking at a work of art.

Art is often viewed as a powerful form of expression, where even a single brushstroke can unveil hidden depths of energy and emotion. This highlights the significance of how design elements are arranged to convey feelings and impact. Similarly, it is understood that a truly compelling artwork is not simply the result of following set rules but rather the harmonious integration of all its components into a unified whole. This is the core of effective composition—crafting a complete, purposeful, and profoundly expressive piece.

In the design context, composition is not merely about arranging visible elements but also how each part supports and enhances the others. A successful composition interweaves various elements, ensuring they complement each other, resulting in a unified whole that is more significant than the sum of its parts. Achieving this balance gives a design its impact, making it resonate with its audience.

To master composition, a designer must develop the ability to arrange fundamental elements thoughtfully in a personal and harmonious way. The key lies in achieving a sense of completeness, where each component serves its purpose within the overall design. Successful compositions arise from presenting artistic elements in varied yet cohesive ways, always considering the artwork as a unified entity.

TYPES OF COMPOSITIONS:

Classical Composition: This type focuses on centralizing the primary subject within the artwork. The most significant elements are often positioned at or near the center, creating a self-contained composition that feels resolved within its boundaries. The focus remains entirely on the central theme, providing a clear and direct visual experience.

Decorative Composition: In contrast, open compositions extend beyond the confines of the artwork, as if the design elements continue beyond the edges of the frame. This approach allows shapes and forms to flow freely, creating a balanced yet unrestricted arrangement. Decorative compositions are commonly seen in modern art, where the design intentionally spills beyond traditional borders, inviting the viewer to imagine the continuation beyond what is visible.

05

DESIGN ELEMENTS

1. POINT-LINE:

23

Point:

A "point" is fundamental to teaching artistic principles and elements. It can be expanded, contracted, or diversified. The point is the simplest design element and represents the starting point for creating volume and dimension. A line is formed from the moment's movement, and planes and surfaces emerge.

When arranged, a single point can convey a sense of tranquility or stillness. However, when points are scattered or grouped, they can suggest motion or dynamic energy. Points can grow in size, shrink, or change direction, leading to various compositions and visual arrangements.

Depending on their arrangement, a composition of points can evoke feelings of order or chaos. When points are organized methodically, they create harmonious and balanced surfaces. In contrast, irregularly scattered points can generate visual tension or dynamic contrasts.

When evenly distributed on a surface, individually placed points can produce a calm, soothing effect. However, variations in the density of points—whether they increase or decrease across a surface—affect the interplay of light and shadow, fostering a sense of depth or texture. This effect is achieved by manipulating the spacing and density of the points.

A radial arrangement of points, starting from the center and expanding outward, creates a feeling of dispersion. Conversely, converging points toward the center evoke a sense of gathering or cohesion. Altering the direction of points on a surface can also create a sense of movement or flow.

In everyday life, the point is a universal and widely recognized element in both written language and artistic forms. Beyond its practical applications, the point carries symbolic meanings in our emotional lives, often signifying an end or a new beginning. Everything starts with a point, which is why it is the first element introduced in the study of Basic Design.

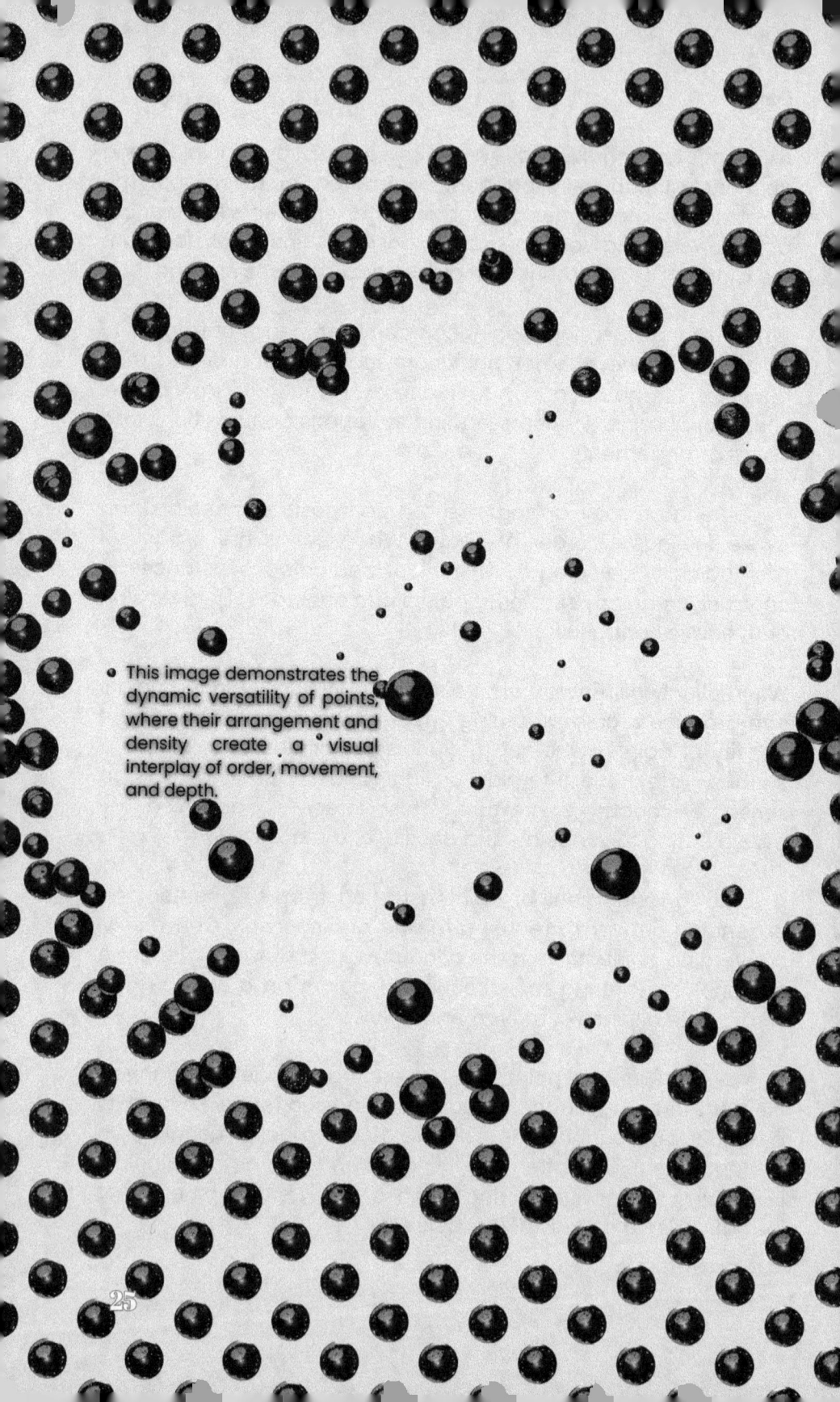
This image demonstrates the dynamic versatility of points, where their arrangement and density create a visual interplay of order, movement, and depth.

This image demonstrates the dynamic versatility of points, where their arrangement and density create a visual interplay of order, movement, and depth.

TASK

1. Point Composition Exploration: Create a series of compositions using only points. Experiment with varying sizes, densities, and arrangements to convey emotions or movements. This exercise enhances sensitivity to how point placement affects visual perception.
2. Environmental Point Identification: Observe and document instances of points in your surroundings, such as patterns in architecture, nature, or textiles. Photograph or sketch these observations to understand how points function in various contexts.
3. Pointillism Technique Application: Develop a simple image or pattern using the pointillism technique, where numerous small dots create the overall form. This practice improves precision and appreciation for how individual points interact to form a cohesive image.
4. Emotional Expression Through Points: Design compositions that use only points to express specific emotions (e.g., calmness, chaos). Manipulate factors like spacing, size, and distribution to convey the intended feeling.
5. Collaborative Point Mural: Work with peers to create a large-scale mural of points. Assign sections to each participant, focusing on how individual contributions integrate into a unified design.

Line:

The line is a crucial element in visual storytelling. Art begins with the line. It serves as a fundamental concept in teaching the basics of visual communication and expression. Everything we observe is defined through lines, which give form and artistic meaning to what we see. A line can be considered a one-dimensional element, with varying lengths and thicknesses depending on the material used to draw it.

Humans use The line extensively to express their emotions, ideas, and perceptions visually. Every object is encased in contours that define its shape. When shapes are combined to form a meaningful whole and are infused with artistic value, they transform into compositions. The different lines, whether indicating direction, space, or various measurements, play a significant role in the design, creating distinctive effects that artists and designers often utilize.

People have always used lines to communicate what they see, feel, and imagine, emphasizing the line's enduring importance in art. Lines are essential visual communication tools, expressing thoughts and emotions that words cannot always convey. They help bring our thoughts to life, which is crucial in visual comprehension and interpretation.

In design, lines unify elements and separate, organize, or disrupt existing harmony. Within a composition, lines guide the viewer's eye, establish balance, and introduce a sense of movement and rhythm. The first step in visual communication is often focused on mastering lines. Art begins with lines, making the study of lines fundamental to any form of artistic education.

Art education often starts with lines, teaching students various types such as horizontal, vertical, diagonal, curved, broken, and calligraphic lines. Each type's unique impact contributes to a composition's overall aesthetic and function.

This image showcases lines as fundamental elements of visual communication, where movement, rhythm, and form are harmoniously combined. Lines not only define structure but also depict emotions and thoughts.

This image highlights the power of lines in creating structure and harmony. The geometric patterns, defined by sharp and dynamic lines, illustrate how design combines direction and form to communicate visually.

TASK

1. Blind Contour Drawing: Outline an object without looking at your paper, focusing solely on its contours. This practice enhances hand-eye coordination and trains you to observe details meticulously.
2. Gesture Drawing: Quickly sketch subjects in motion, capturing their essence quickly. This exercise improves your ability to depict movement and fluidity in your designs.
3. Line Variation Studies: Experiment with different line types—such as thick, thin, dashed, and wavy—to understand how each influences the perception of a composition. This helps convey various textures and emotions through line work.
4. Environmental Line Observation: Observe and document how lines are used in your surroundings, like in architecture or nature. Sketch these observations to see how lines define spaces and forms in real-world contexts.
5. Collaborative Line Art: Work with peers to create a large-scale drawing using only lines. This fosters teamwork and shows how individual line styles can merge into a cohesive artwork.

2. TONE-LIGHT-SHADOW-VALUE

36

Colors reveal their actual value when seen in the light spectrum. As each color moves closer to white, it becomes brighter, while approaching black results in a deeper, darker shade. The degree of lightness or darkness of a color is referred to as "tone." This tonal value (often called "value" in art) represents lightness or darkness perceived on objects under illumination. The general term used to describe this is "tone." When examining objects illuminated by different light sources, four primary tone levels emerge: light tone, medium tone, dark tone, and shadow, which also has light-dark gradations.

As a color transitions from light to shadow, it undergoes tonal gradations known as value changes. This variation shows how light or dark a color will appear when exposed to sunlight or cast in shadow. However, the interplay of light and shadow is closely linked to using warm and cool colors in a painting. The elements of tone, value, and contrast are essential in creating depth, adding the illusion of the third dimension, and enhancing the sense of space in the artwork.

Nature forms complex compositions through infinite combinations of tone, color, shape, and countless variations. In nature, forms, spaces, and values are interwoven. The world is a canvas covered in endless layers of tones. For an artist, achieving the correct tonal value is essential, whether through drawing, shading, or painting. Colors create shapes, forms, and surfaces that result in harmonious compositions. The two core components, value, and color, are vital elements in an artwork's composition.

Artists use tonal values to enhance emphasis in their work, create depth illusions, and add dimensionality to objects on the canvas. In compositions, the strategic use of value contributes significantly to conveying light and shadow, ensuring a balanced interplay between these elements. Understanding how to manipulate value enables artists to achieve vibrant contrasts and dynamic compositions, giving life and realism to their subjects.

The photograph captures the intricate play of light, shadow, and tonal gradations, illustrating the transition from brightness to darkness. This dynamic interaction emphasizes depth and dimensionality, showcasing how tonal values define space and form in the natural world.

TASK

1. Value Scale Creation: Draw a series of squares transitioning from pure white to deep black, including various shades of gray in between. This practice enhances your ability to discern subtle differences between light and dark.
2. Grayscale Observation: Select a colored image and recreate it using only shades of gray. This exercise helps us understand how colors translate into values, emphasizing the importance of light and dark over hue.
3. Chiaroscuro Studies: Focus on the interplay of light and shadow by drawing simple objects with a single light source—this technique, known as chiaroscuro, aids in modeling three-dimensional forms on a two-dimensional surface.
4. Tonal Composition Analysis: Examine artworks that effectively use tonal contrast to create depth and focus. Identify the range of values employed and consider how they guide the viewer's eye through the composition.
5. Practical Application: Apply your understanding of tonal values in a new piece, consciously utilizing a range of tones to build form and emphasize critical elements. Reflect on how this deliberate use of value enhances the overall impact of your artwork.

3. TEXTURE

When you touch the surface of a painting, you can feel its texture, which also gives a visual depth. The general understanding of texture refers to the surface quality of an object. Nature surrounds us with various surfaces, each with its distinct texture that we can perceive visually and through touch. Every element in a painting reflects a unique surface quality that distinguishes it.

Texture can have diverse properties, such as rough, smooth, or soft. These characteristics can be visually perceived even when you don't touch the object. Textures enrich the depth and impact of a composition. For instance, the texture of a material significantly affects how light and shadow play on its surface, altering the perception of depth.

While some classical artists, like Masaccio and Piero della Francesca, focused on creating depth without emphasizing texture, later movements like Impressionism began to explore texture more deeply. Before the Impressionists, the concept of texture was less widely studied. The Impressionists discovered the power of texture and started to use it extensively to convey visual energy.

Modern artists, who integrated texture deliberately into their compositions, made the conscious use of texture more prominent. For example, artists used texture to depict objects' surface quality and add emotional resonance. In a painting, combining various textures can evoke different feelings and create a more immersive experience.

Textures are crucial in adding depth and richness to visual art and serve as powerful tools for enhancing the tactile experience of a piece. Whether smooth or rough, textures engage the viewer's senses and draw them closer to the work, making it more dynamic and compelling.

Understanding texture is essential in designing visually appealing compositions that captivate the viewer. Whether used subtly to enhance a background or boldly to define a focal point, texture plays a fundamental role in a design's overall impact.

TEXTURE IN ART AND DESIGN

Texture is an element extensively used in the visual arts. When you touch a surface, the sensation you experience can vary—it may feel smooth, soft like satin, or rough and grainy. In a visual context, texture conveys more than just a tactile feeling; it brings depth and dimension to a piece. By observing how light reflects off a textured surface, one can perceive whether it is smooth, uneven, or rough.

Natural Textures are formed due to natural processes inherent to the objects they cover. These textures can be observed on rocks, leaves, wood, or animal hides. Natural textures are not random; they display a coherent pattern and structure. For instance, the texture of a tree bark or a leaf is visually and tactilely distinct, providing unique qualities to each object. Natural textures are typically irregular, yet they possess an organic harmony that reflects the intricate growth processes of nature.

Artificial Textures are artificial. These are created through artistic interpretation and techniques, using materials like paint, metal, or glass to replicate or reinterpret natural textures. Artists often use artificial textures to express their creativity, applying brushstrokes, spatulas, or other tools to mimic or enhance the natural feel of objects. Artificial textures are not merely a replication but a transformation, turning a flat surface into one that feels alive and dynamic.

Integrating texture into a composition enriches visual appeal and influences the viewer's emotional response. By varying textures, artists can create contrasts, draw attention to specific areas, or evoke particular feelings, thereby enhancing the overall impact of their work.

Texture in design is not limited to what we can physically touch. It also involves what the eye perceives. Texture is crucial in bringing objects to life in two-dimensional and three-dimensional works. Whether through the graininess of a rough surface or the smooth reflection of a polished one, texture invites the viewer to explore and engage with the piece on a deeper level.

Natural Textures

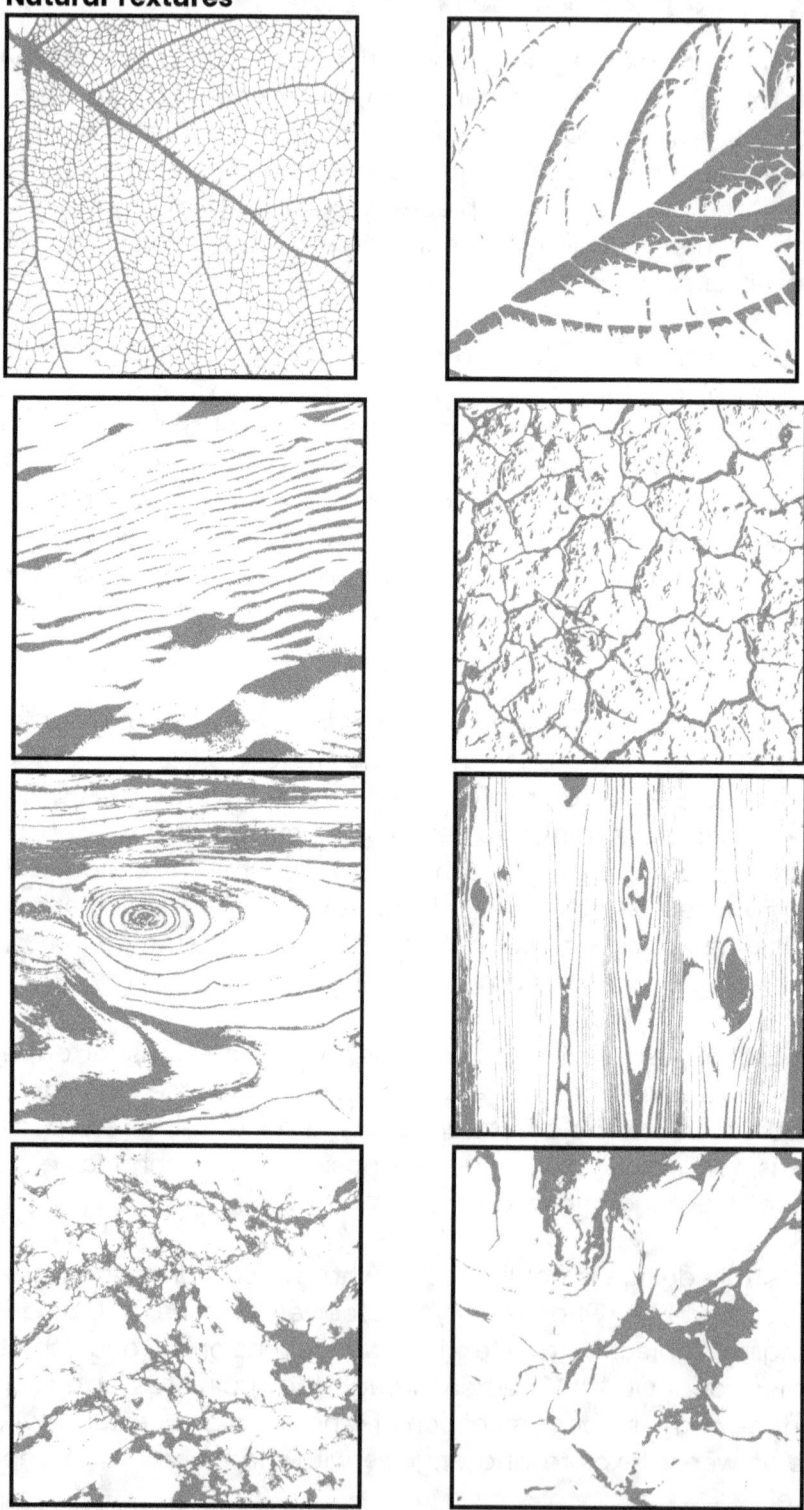

Artificial Textures

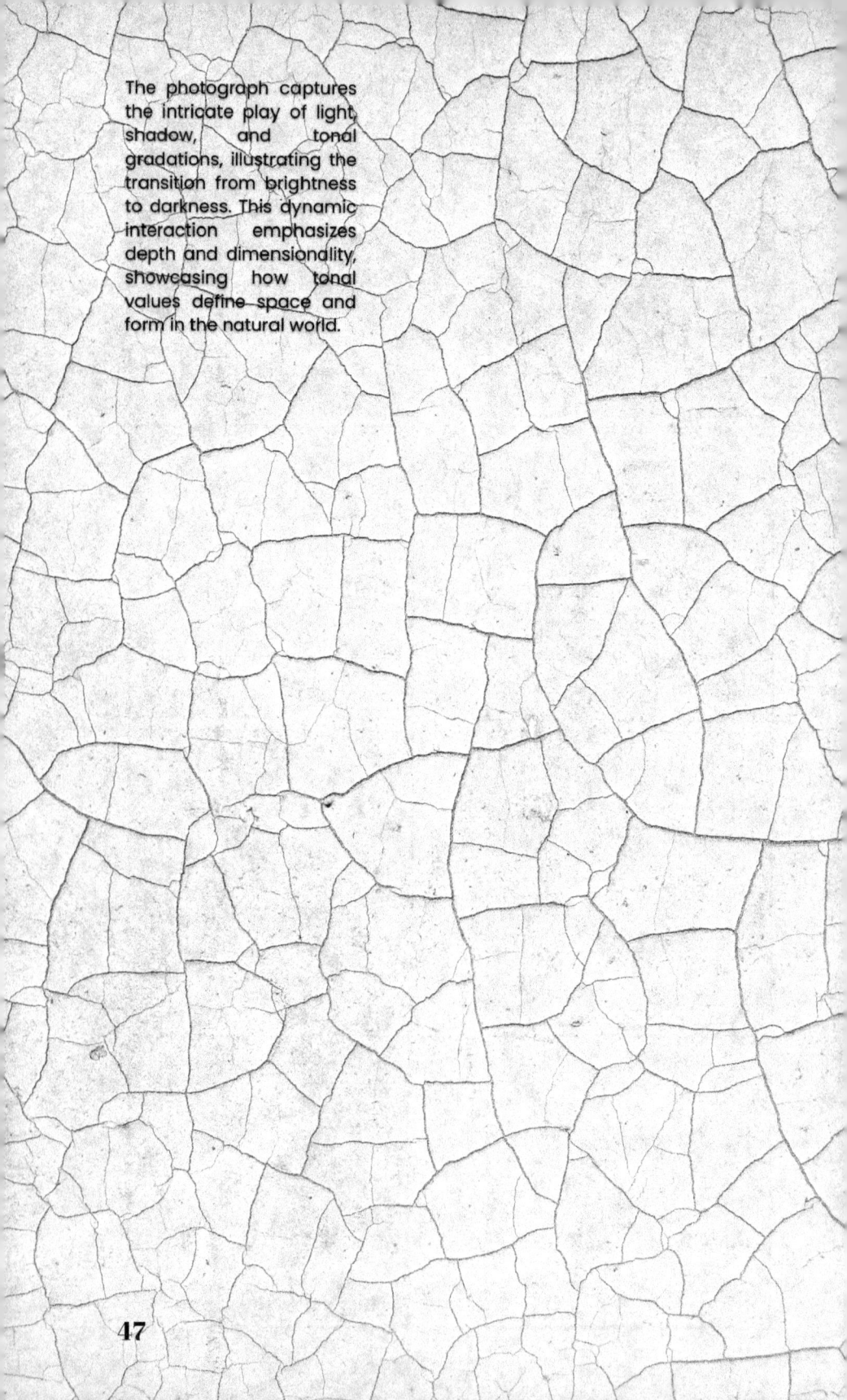

The photograph captures the intricate play of light, shadow, and tonal gradations, illustrating the transition from brightness to darkness. This dynamic interaction emphasizes depth and dimensionality, showcasing how tonal values define space and form in the natural world.

This image illustrates the vibrant beauty of artificial textures, where artistic techniques transform a flat surface into a dynamic and lively expression of creativity.

TASK

1. Value Scale Creation: Draw a series of squares transitioning from pure white to deep black, including various shades of gray in between. This practice enhances your ability to discern subtle differences between light and dark.
2. Grayscale Observation: Select a colored image and recreate it using only shades of gray. This exercise helps us understand how colors translate into values, emphasizing the importance of light and dark over hue.
3. Chiaroscuro Studies: Focus on the interplay of light and shadow by drawing simple objects with a single light source—this technique, known as chiaroscuro, aids in modeling three-dimensional forms on a two-dimensional surface.
4. Tonal Composition Analysis: Examine artworks that effectively use tonal contrast to create depth and focus. Could you identify the range of values employed and consider how they guide the viewer's eye through the composition?
5. Practical Application: Apply your understanding of tonal values in a new piece, consciously utilizing a range of tones to build form and emphasize critical elements. Reflect on how this deliberate use of value enhances the overall impact of your artwork.

4. COLOR

Colors are inseparable from our daily lives. They influence our emotions, thoughts, and perceptions of the world. In design and art, color is one of the most powerful tools for conveying emotions, creating ambiance, and drawing attention. The psychological effects of color are profound, making it essential for any designer to understand its impact.

Color exists because of light and changes with the amount and type of light it reflects. The perception of color is directly linked to how light interacts with an object. Without light, colors cannot exist. As light changes throughout the day, so do the colors we perceive, shifting with different intensities and tones.

Color in compositions is critical for creating harmony (balance). Colors can complement each other to achieve unity or contrast to create visual interest. Understanding how to manipulate color allows designers to guide the viewer's eye, emphasize elements, or set the mood within a composition. Bright, vibrant colors evoke energy and excitement, while muted, darker tones convey seriousness or calmness.

In nature, colors change with the seasons, reflecting different moods and atmospheres. The colors we see in autumn differ vastly from those in spring or winter, each carrying its unique energy. Designers and artists often draw inspiration from these natural palettes to bring depth and relatability to their work.

By understanding the relationship between light and color, artists can create illusions of depth, texture, and dimension on a two-dimensional plane. This skill is fundamental in achieving a realistic or stylized representation within a design. The strategic use of colors and awareness of their psychological and emotional impact can elevate a design from mere visual communication to a powerful experience that resonates with its audience.

Color is not just about aesthetics; it's about meaning, symbolism, and psychological influence. The colors used in any work of art or design can subtly (or boldly) alter the viewer's perception, guiding their emotions and responses to the piece. Thus, mastering the art of color theory and its application is crucial for any designer who wants to create impactful, memorable works.

THE COLOR WHEEL

The color wheel represents a fundamental concept in design. It organizes colors in a circular format to illustrate their relationships. It includes three primary colors: red, yellow, and blue, which form the basis of all other hues. These primary colors are arranged within the color wheel at equal distances, creating an equilateral triangle. The result is a system where the primary colors mix to form secondary colors such as green, orange, and purple.

The **color wheel** is a visual tool that helps designers select colors that work well together. The color wheel is divided into three main categories:

The spectrum is the range of visible colors, including red, orange, yellow, green, blue, indigo, and violet, appearing when white light is dispersed. Understanding color interactions and creating harmonious combinations is essential in graphic design and art.

PRIMARY COLORS

The three primary hues at the heart of the color wheel are red, yellow, and blue. These colors cannot be created by blending other colors. Instead, they serve as the source of all different colors.

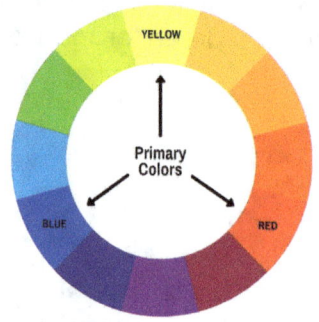

Primary colours
Primary colors make up the basis for the color wheel. Here they are Red, Yellow and Blue.

SECONDARY COLORS

The blending of primary colors leads to the creation of secondary colors. For instance:

- **Blue + Yellow = Green**
- **Red + Yellow = Orange**
- **Blue + Red = Purple**

These secondary colors emerge by mixing equal parts of the primary colors, creating a cohesive color palette essential for any design project.

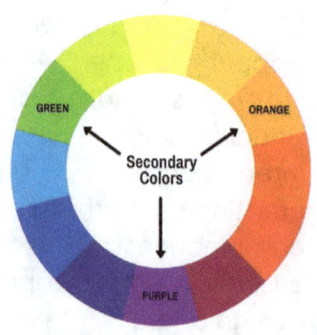

Secondary colorus
Secondary colors are made by mixing equal portions of the primary colors. These create green, orange, and purple.

WARM AND COOL COLORS

The color wheel also categorizes colors as warm or cool based on their psychological impact and visual effects. Warm colors (like red, orange, and yellow) evoke feelings of warmth, energy, and excitement, and they appear to advance or come forward in a composition. On the other hand, cool colors (such as blue, green, and purple) convey calmness, tranquility, and serenity, creating the impression of receding or moving back into space.

Warm & cool colours
Warm colours on the right.
Cool colours on the left

NEUTRAL COLORS

In art and design, neutral colors—black, white, and the grays produced by their combination—are pivotal in creating balanced and harmonious compositions. Often perceived as calm and stable, these tones play a crucial role in emphasizing elements such as tone, value, and chiaroscuro within artworks. By integrating neutral colors, artists can maintain equilibrium in the relationship between color and form, enhancing the impact of other hues in the piece.

Neutral colors can dominate a composition to establish rhythm and impart artistic significance while enabling the artwork to adapt seamlessly to various environmental conditions. Artists explore how these colors interact with time and space to infuse their works with depth and emphasis, ultimately elevating the artistic value and rendering the piece more compelling to the viewer.

CONTRAST COLORS

Contrast colors are those positioned directly opposite each other on the color wheel, creating a stark visual distinction. Examples include:

- **Yellow and Purple**
- **Red and Green**
- **Blue and Orange**

These pairs are chosen because they intensify one another when placed side by side, creating a striking effect. Mix them to determine if the two colors indeed contrast. If the resulting color is a neutral tone like grey or black, they are perfect complementary contrasts.

The design uses contrasting colors to grab attention, create focus, and build a dynamic visual experience. The contrasting hues can guide the viewer's eye across a composition, emphasizing some aspects while enhancing the overall visual impact.

HIGH CONTRAST

MEDIUM CONTRAST

LOW CONTRAST

HARMONIOUS COLORS

In the color wheel, adjacent colors are referred to as harmonious colors. Color harmony involves two or more colors that sit next to each other on the wheel. Harmonious colors' defining characteristic is their ability to create a pleasing and cohesive visual experience. For a composition to be truly effective, it's crucial to understand how colors and their relationships function.

In design, achieving color harmony is one of the primary goals in creating compositions. Harmonious colors are essential in emphasizing the unity of the design elements, ensuring that the viewer's attention is kept where intended. However, using colors that are not harmonious can lead to visual discomfort and disrupt the intended impact of the piece.

In this context, mastering color harmony is one of the first challenges to tackle in the early stages of design education. This is not just an academic exercise but a critical skill that influences how a design is perceived, ensuring that the viewer experiences the intended message in the most aesthetically pleasing way.

RULES OF COLOR HARMONY

Effective use of colors in design requires a good understanding of color combination rules. Some of these rules include:

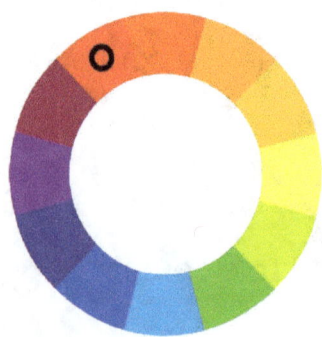

1. Monochromatic Colors: These consist of shades and tones of a single color and usually create balanced and soothing compositions. Monochromatic color schemes contribute to visual unity and simplicity in design.

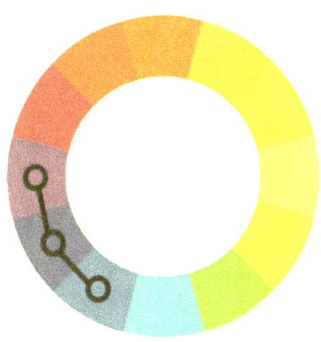

2. Analogous Colors:

These colors are located close to each other on the color wheel and typically create harmonious and exciting combinations. Analogous colors often have a natural harmony and can effectively create visually appealing and complex designs.

3. Complementary Colors:

These opposite colors on the color wheel create high contrast, leading to vibrant and dynamic compositions. Complementary colors are particularly effective in drawing attention and adding energy to critical areas of the design.

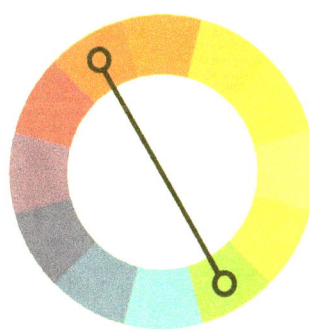

4. Triadic Colors:

These colors are evenly spaced around the color wheel, creating solid and attractive visual effects. Triadic color schemes add diversity and dynamism to a design, making it more engaging for the viewer.

TASK

1. Color Emotion Chart Creation
Objective: Develop a personal reference chart that associates colors with the emotions they commonly evoke.
Instructions:
Research the psychological effects of various colors.
Create a chart or wheel displaying colors alongside their corresponding emotional responses.
Reflect on how these associations might vary across different cultures or contexts.
Outcome: This exercise will enhance your ability to select colors purposefully to elicit desired emotional responses in your designs.

2. Color Scheme Development for Target Audiences
Objective: Design color palettes tailored to specific demographics or user groups.
Instructions:
Identify a target audience (e.g., children, professionals, seniors).
Research color preferences and psychological responses are typical of that group.
Create a color scheme that aligns with the audience's expectations and emotional triggers.
Outcome: This task will improve your ability to create user-centered designs that effectively communicate with the intended audience.

3. Comparative Analysis of Brand Color Usage
Objective: Analyze how brands utilize color to convey their identity and influence consumer perception.
Instructions:
Select two competing brands.
Examine their color choices in logos, marketing materials, and products.
Assess how these colors support the brand's message and appeal to their target market.
Outcome: This analysis will provide insights into strategic color use in branding and its impact on consumer behavior.

4. Cultural Color Significance Research

Objective: Investigate how different cultures interpret colors and the implications for global design projects.

Instructions:

Please choose a color and research its meanings in various cultural contexts.

Document any significant differences or similarities.

Consider how these insights can inform culturally sensitive design choices.

Outcome: This research will help you create respectful and compelling designs across diverse cultural audiences.

5. Practical Application: Redesign Exercise

Objective: Apply your understanding of color psychology by redesigning an existing advertisement or webpage.

Instructions:

Select an advertisement or webpage.

Analyze its current color scheme and the emotions it conveys.

Redesign the piece using a different color palette to alter its emotional impact.

Outcome: This practical application will demonstrate how color adjustments can change the perception and effectiveness of a design.

5. STAIN

A stain covers a design surface using space, texture, shape, and depth to create a specific visual expression. The concept of "stain" was first introduced in the 1950s by a French art critic who emphasized its connection to abstract and expressionist movements. Stain involves creating a sense of texture, tone, and visual feel on a surface, allowing for differentiation through its visible and tactile properties. It can be achieved using various materials like paint, texture, or light-shadow techniques.

The stain can be applied to surfaces to create tonal or textural effects, making it one of the most impactful elements of visual communication. In its most basic artistic sense, a stain refers to traces of paint applied to a surface. Brush strokes are an example of this approach. When applied uniformly, a stain is a fundamental component of a painting, covering the surface uniformly. It acts as a layer that wraps the surface, transforming it from a blank canvas to a textured, expressive entity.

Stains are not just about color but can carry emotional and functional significance. For example, they can enhance the design motif, adding depth and texture to the artwork. The stain is essential in visual perception, affecting how the viewer interprets and interacts with the artwork. The tactile feel of a surface covered with stains can convey softness or roughness or even create a sense of volume and form.

In visual arts, stains emphasize certain aspects of the composition, drawing the viewer's attention and guiding the eye. For instance, a smooth and continuous stain can create a sense of calm, while a rough, textured stain can evoke energy and tension. In design exercises, using stains can teach creators how to manipulate visual weight, balance, and focus within a composition.

Ultimately, the stain is an expressive tool that covers and communicates, transforming the surface into a visual storytelling medium.

This image highlights the expressive power of stains, where texture, tone, and depth transform a blank surface into a compelling visual narrative.

TASK

1. Stain Application Exploration: Experiment with various materials —such as ink, watercolor, or diluted acrylics—to create stains on different surfaces like paper, canvas, or fabric. Observe how each medium interacts with the surface, noting differences in absorption, spread, and texture. This will help you understand how stains can alter a design's visual and tactile qualities.

2. Texture Creation Through Staining: Use staining techniques to develop a range of textures, from smooth gradients to rough, uneven surfaces. Apply washes of color in varying intensities to see how they can simulate textures such as wood grain, stone, or fabric. This practice will enhance your ability to convey different material qualities in your designs.

3. Emotional Expression with Stains: Create compositions where stains are the primary method of expression. Experiment with color choices, application methods, and intensity to evoke specific emotions or moods, such as calmness, chaos, warmth, or coldness. This exercise will help you understand the emotional impact of stains in visual communication.

4. Stain Integration in Mixed Media: Combine staining techniques with other artistic methods like drawing, collage, or digital art. Explore how stains can serve as backgrounds, focal points, or unifying elements within a mixed-media composition. This will develop your skill in integrating stains cohesively into diverse design projects.

5. Historical Analysis of Stain Techniques: Research artists are known for using stains, such as Helen Frankenthaler with her soak-stain method. Analyze how these artists employed stains to achieve specific aesthetic effects and how their techniques can inform your practice. This study will provide context and inspiration for your use of stains in design.

6. SHAPE, FORM, AND DIMENSION

Shape is the arrangement of visual elements that are creatively organized to form a cohesive whole. It plays a crucial role in visual communication, serving as one of the fundamental tools used to convey meaning within a design. We use two-dimensional and three-dimensional elements alongside various techniques to achieve the intended visual impact in creative applications. Geometric forms and configurations are often the basis for shaping objects and transforming figures into artistic forms.

Two-dimensional shapes are generally based on geometric forms, while three-dimensional ones include volumes that can be perceived in space. Shapes and forms can be classified into two main categories:

- Geometric Forms follow specific, calculated patterns and configurations, often exhibiting sharp, defined edges. Examples include squares, circles, triangles, and polygons. Geometric forms lend themselves to designs where precision and order are essential.
- Organic Forms: These shapes are more fluid and irregular, inspired by natural elements like plants, animals, and free-flowing curves. Organic forms often appear softer and more harmonious, creating a sense of natural movement within a composition.

In creative fields, distinguishing between shape and form is crucial, even though they are often used interchangeably. While shapes are typically two-dimensional, forms have volume and can be perceived in three dimensions. For instance, a shape may consist of only a surface with height and width, whereas a form encompasses depth as well, giving the object a tangible presence.

Understanding the relationship between form, background, and composition is critical when working with shapes. This relationship directly impacts how viewers perceive depth, space, and visual weight within a design.

Forms in nature are not limited to rigid geometric structures; they can blend geometric and organic characteristics. For example, many organic forms have geometric tendencies, like the patterns found in honeycombs or the symmetry of leaves. Recognizing this blend can enhance the creative process, providing a deeper understanding of balancing rigidity and fluidity in design.

Finally, three-dimensionality is essential in fields such as sculpture, architecture, and industrial design, where the physicality of objects is a core element. However, even in two-dimensional artworks like paintings, artists can create the illusion of depth using shading, perspective, and overlapping forms.

This image illustrates the interplay of geometric and organic forms, where precise patterns meet fluid curves to create a harmonious visual composition.

TASK

- Geometric vs. Organic Shape Exploration: Create a series of sketches that distinguish between geometric shapes (like squares, circles, triangles) and organic shapes (such as free-form, naturalistic designs). This will help you recognize and apply different forms in your compositions.
- 2D to 3D Transformation: Start with basic two-dimensional shapes and practice transforming them into three-dimensional forms by adding depth through perspective and shading. For example, turn a square into a cube or a circle into a sphere. This exercise enhances your ability to visualize and render forms in space.
- Positive and Negative Space Studies: Draw a simple object, focusing on the object itself (positive space) and the space around it (negative space). Understanding the balance between these spaces is crucial for effective composition.
- Form and Light Interaction: Set up primary forms like cubes, spheres, and cylinders under a light source. Draw these forms, closely examining how light and shadow define their three-dimensionality. This practice will improve your shading skills and understanding of volume.
- Mixed Media Shape Collage: Use various materials (paper, fabric, etc.) to create a collage that combines geometric and organic shapes. This tactile approach will deepen your comprehension of how different forms interact and coexist in a composition.

7. SPACE AND FULLNESS

In art and design, achieving balance within a composition is both an art and a science. The challenge lies in arranging elements harmoniously yet dynamically, avoiding the pitfalls of static or monotonous designs that fail to engage the viewer. The solution often lies in the strategic use of contrast, which introduces variety and movement to the composition. Designers can create captivating and cohesive works by carefully adjusting scale, spacing, and intervals. This approach ensures the composition is visually appealing and emotionally resonant, drawing the viewer into an engaging visual experience. The Principle of Space and Fullness is a cornerstone of achieving this balance. It focuses on the interplay between presence and absence, between densely packed areas with visual elements, and intentionally left open. This equilibrium is essential in creating a sense of rhythm and movement, allowing the composition to breathe while guiding the viewer's eye to key focal points. Space provides calm and clarity, while fullness delivers intensity and focus. Together, they create a dialogue that brings the artwork to life, making it feel vibrant and intentional.

Compelling compositions are built on contrasts—between light and shadow, large and small, dense and open. Thoughtfully leaving some areas unoccupied while enriching others establishes a visual hierarchy, directing attention where it is most needed. This balance transforms a design from merely functional to deeply impactful, imbuing it with layers of depth, intrigue, and meaning. The psychological impact of this balance cannot be overstated; open spaces evoke tranquility and simplicity, while filled areas suggest energy and activity. Designers must be mindful of these effects, tailoring their use of space and fullness to align with the intended message and emotion of the piece. Consistency with the overall design vision is paramount to applying this principle effectively. Each decision, from the placement of elements to the manipulation of color, light, and shadow, should serve the composition's narrative. Open areas should not feel empty; instead, they should act as intentional pauses that enhance the flow of the design. Similarly, densely filled areas should not overwhelm but instead anchor the composition, providing contrast and interest. The goal is to ensure that every element contributes to the overall story the design seeks to tell.

Mastery of the Principle of Space and Fullness empowers designers to elevate their work, turning ordinary arrangements into extraordinary artistic expressions. When this principle is applied with skill, the resulting composition is pleasing to the eye and memorable, leaving a lasting impression on the viewer. It draws them in, encourages exploration, and evokes emotion. By embracing the delicate interplay of space and fullness, designers can craft works that resonate on both a visual and emotional level, achieving a balance that is as impactful as it is beautiful.

Whether in architecture, graphic design, or fine art, this principle transcends disciplines, offering a universal guide to creating compositions rich in aesthetic brilliance and artistic depth. Through thoughtful application, designers can unlock new dimensions in their work, pushing boundaries and achieving striking and timeless results.

This image exemplifies the principle of space and fullness, where the interplay between dense structures and open areas creates a dynamic and harmonious visual balance.

TASK

1. Dynamic Balance Exercise:
   - Create two compositions:
     - One with a dominant use of fullness, where most of the space is densely filled.
     - Another focusing on space, where most of the design emphasizes openness.
   - Use simple shapes (e.g., circles, squares, lines) and arrange them on a blank canvas (digital or paper).
   - Reflect on how the balance (or imbalance) affects the composition's mood and visual flow.
2. Contrast Exploration:
   - Design a piece that contrasts light and shadow, large and small, or dense and open spaces.
   - Experiment with different intervals and placements of elements to create rhythm and guide the viewer's eye.
   - Write a short paragraph explaining how your choices contribute to the overall harmony and emotional impact of the design.
3. Narrative Composition:
   - Develop a composition that tells a story or conveys a specific emotion (e.g., tranquility, excitement).
   - Use the principle of space and fullness to highlight key focal points and create movement within the piece.
   - Could you share your work with peers or friends and gather feedback on whether the composition effectively conveys your intended narrative?
4. Photography Assignment:
   - Take 3 photographs of everyday environments (e.g., a crowded marketplace, an empty park, or a minimalistic interior).
   - Analyze the use of space and fullness in each photo:
     - Identify areas of contrast between dense and open spaces.
     - Reflect on how these contrasts influence the composition's visual appeal and emotional tone.

8. DIRECTION

In the art of design, direction is a fundamental component that shapes how compositions communicate and guide the viewer's eye. Using lines, points, and various elements, designers craft a sense of movement, ensuring the composition feels purposeful and dynamic. Direction establishes flow, providing a structured pathway for the viewer to explore the visual narrative, and it transforms static elements into engaging, active components of the design.

Direction can manifest as horizontal, vertical, or diagonal, each evoking unique psychological and visual responses. Horizontal directions convey stability and calm, grounding the viewer in balance, while vertical directions suggest growth, aspiration, and hierarchy. On the other hand, diagonal directions introduce energy and vibrancy, creating tension and movement that inject life into the composition. These directions are often defined by the placement and orientation of lines and shapes, which naturally lead the eye toward focal points and areas of emphasis.

When incorporating direction into a design, aligning it with the intended message or emotional tone is essential. Clear direction highlights areas of focus and brings rhythm and flow, ensuring the piece feels cohesive and deliberate. Active directions, like bold diagonals, evoke energy and dynamism, while passive directions, such as soft horizontals, provide balance and moments of rest. The interplay between these directions gives depth and harmony to the overall composition.

A well-considered sense of direction elevates a design from visually appealing to profoundly compelling. It allows the viewer to observe and experience the work, following intentional pathways that reinforce the design's narrative and emotional impact. Mastery of direction ensures the composition is seen and felt, leaving a lasting impression that resonates deeply with the audience.

This image illustrates the power of direction in design, where dynamic lines and pathways guide the viewer's eye, creating movement and an engaging visual narrative.

TASK

1. Line Direction Exploration:
   - Create three separate compositions, each emphasizing a different direction:
     - Horizontal Direction: Convey a sense of balance and calm using horizontal lines and elements.
     - Vertical Direction: Highlight growth, elevation, or hierarchy through vertical arrangements.
     - Diagonal Direction: Introduce energy and dynamism with diagonal lines and shapes.
   - Develop these compositions using basic shapes and lines on paper or a digital platform.
2. Direction and Emotion:
   - Design a piece that utilizes direction to evoke a specific emotion (e.g., excitement, tranquility, tension).
   - Write a brief paragraph explaining how the directional elements contribute to the desired emotional tone.
3. Narrative Flow:
   - Create a visual story or sequence that guides the viewer's eye from one part of the composition to another using direction.
   - Employ lines, shapes, and spacing to establish a clear visual pathway.
   - Assess whether the viewer can intuitively follow the narrative.
4. Photography Assignment:
   - Capture or find three photographs that naturally demonstrate horizontal, vertical, and diagonal directions in real-life settings.
   - Analyze each image:
     - Determine how the directional elements influence the viewer's focus.
     - Discuss how the direction contributes to the mood or flow of the composition.
5. Collaborative Project (Optional):
   - Collaborate with a group to design a large-scale mural or poster that uses different directions to create distinct zones of focus and movement.
   - Assign each participant a directional style (horizontal, vertical, diagonal) and ensure their sections integrate cohesively.

BASIC DESIGN PRINCIPLES

The principles of design are the foundation that forms the structure of any visual composition. These principles guide how elements are arranged to create a cohesive and balanced design, ultimately giving form to a piece of art. The design process involves organizing forms, building structure, and establishing harmony among the elements. Throughout the design process, whether it's shaping forms, using specific components, or setting up a layout, the principles are critical in determining the artistic outcome of the work.

These principles are versatile; they can be applied across various fields, whether in art, design, or even architecture, reflecting a timeless set of guidelines that enrich any creative work. It's important to note that design principles are not rigid rules but flexible concepts that allow creative exploration. In our discussion of design, we define eight fundamental principles:

- **Repetition**
- **Balance and Rhythm**
- **Harmony**
- **Proportion and Scale**
- **Unity**
- **Space**
- **Emphasis and Dominance**
- **Contrast and Variation**

Each principle serves a specific purpose in enhancing a design's visual impact and effectiveness. By understanding and applying these principles, designers can create compositions that are aesthetically pleasing and convey meaning and purpose effectively.

1. REPETITION

Repetition uses a design element multiple times in a composition to create rhythm, continuity, and visual harmony. By repeating elements such as shapes, colors, textures, or patterns, designers can establish a sense of cohesion that ties the composition together, making it feel balanced and purposeful. This principle not only strengthens the unity of a design but also guides the viewer's eye, directing attention and fostering an intuitive understanding of the visual flow.

In practice, repetition can take many forms, from simple and consistent replication of an element to more dynamic applications involving variations in scale, orientation, or color. For example, a repeated shape might gradually increase in size to emphasize movement toward a focal point, or alternating colors within a repeated pattern might add vibrancy and depth to the design. These variations introduce a sense of rhythm that prevents monotony while maintaining a unified structure.

The spacing between repeated elements is equally significant, affecting how the viewer perceives rhythm and movement. Tight, regular intervals can create a feeling of order and stability, while irregular or varied spacing introduces dynamism and energy. Repetition thus becomes a versatile tool, allowing designers to convey messages ranging from calm and balance to excitement and tension, depending on how it is applied.

Beyond aesthetics, repetition functions in design by emphasizing essential elements and reinforcing the visual hierarchy. For instance, a recurring logo or graphic in a layout enhances brand recognition and ensures consistency across different design pieces. Similarly, repetition in architectural spaces, such as columns or patterns, can create a sense of grandeur and continuity while guiding movement.

Repetition is a powerful principle that balances variety with unity, enabling designers to achieve aesthetic appeal and functional clarity. Its practical use depends on the designer's intent and the message they wish to communicate, making it an indispensable tool for crafting meaningful and engaging visual experiences.

This image highlights the principle of repetition, where recurring geometric patterns create a rhythmic harmony, blending unity with visual dynamism.

This image exemplifies the principle of repetition, where layered patterns create a rhythmic flow, blending order and visual harmony seamlessly.

TASK

1. Repetition in Shapes:
   - Create a composition using a single shape repeated multiple times.
   - Experiment with variations in size, spacing, and orientation to observe how these changes influence rhythm and visual flow.
2. Pattern Creation:
   - Design a seamless pattern using two or more design elements (shapes, colors, or textures).
   - Ensure the pattern maintains consistency while introducing subtle variations for dynamism.
3. Repetition in Real Life:
   - Photograph three examples of repetition in your surroundings (e.g., tiled floors, rows of windows, or fences).
   - Analyze how repetition contributes to the overall design and function of the objects.
4. Creating Visual Hierarchy:
   - Design a poster where repetition highlights vital elements and establishes a visual hierarchy.
   - Use repeated elements to guide the viewer's attention and emphasize the primary message.
5. Interactive Group Project (Optional):
   - Collaborate with peers to create a mural or large-scale artwork where repetition is used as the dominant design principle.
   - Assign each participant a specific element (shape, color, or texture) to repeat, ensuring the final piece is cohesive and engaging.

2. BALANCE AND RHYTHM

BBalance in design is a cornerstone aesthetic principle that establishes a sense of harmony and visual stability within a composition. It ensures that all parts of the design relate cohesively, enabling the viewer to experience the piece as a unified whole. Balance organizes visual elements in a natural and satisfying way, encouraging the eye to navigate the composition seamlessly. It can manifest as symmetrical, asymmetrical, or radial, each serving unique purposes and eliciting distinct emotional responses.

Symmetrical balance, where elements on either side of a central axis mirror each other, creates a sense of formality and order, making it ideal for designs requiring a structured and authoritative tone. Asymmetrical balance, by contrast, relies on strategically placing elements of differing sizes, colors, or shapes to achieve harmony. This approach feels dynamic and contemporary, adding energy and movement while maintaining visual equilibrium. Radial balance radiates outward from a central point and generates a circular flow that naturally draws the viewer's attention inward, often used in designs that emphasize a focal element.

The concept of rhythm complements balance by introducing a sense of movement and continuity within the design. Through the repetition of shapes, colors, textures, or patterns at regular or varied intervals, rhythm creates a flow that guides the viewer's eye across the composition. For instance, repeating curves evoke a calming motion, while bold, repetitive diagonals inject energy and direction into the design. The spacing and arrangement of these repetitions determine the rhythm's impact, from subtle continuity to bold dynamism.

When rhythm and balance are skillfully combined, they establish a dynamic equilibrium that enhances the design's visual appeal and narrative strength. The designer's challenge lies in ensuring these elements complement rather than compete with one another. For example, rhythm can emphasize focal points, while balance ensures that no single element overwhelms the composition. Together, they create a harmonious interplay that captivates the viewer and reinforces the intended message, making them fundamental tools in design.

This image reflects the harmony of balance and rhythm, where the repeating arrangement of plants creates visual stability and a soothing flow.

TASK

1. Symmetrical, Asymmetrical, and Radial Balance
   - Create three separate compositions to demonstrate:
     - Symmetrical Balance: Mirror elements across a central axis.
     - Asymmetrical Balance: Achieve harmony using different sizes, colors, or shapes.
     - Radial Balance: Design elements radiating outward from a central point.
   - Experiment with shapes, colors, and textures to understand the emotional and visual impact of each balance type.
2. Combining Rhythm with Balance
   - Design a composition where rhythm enhances balance.
   - Use repetition of shapes, lines, or colors to create movement while maintaining harmony.
3. Real-Life Observation
   - Photograph or sketch three examples of balance (symmetrical, asymmetrical, and radial) found in everyday surroundings.
   - Analyze the role of balance in these examples and how it contributes to their visual stability.
4. Dynamic Design Experiment
   - Create a poster or digital artwork combining bold rhythmic patterns with balanced elements.
   - Focus on guiding the viewer's attention to a central focal point.
5. Collaborative Design Project (Optional)
   - Work with a group to create a mural or digital artwork that integrates balance and rhythm.
   - Assign roles (e.g., symmetrical balance, rhythm creation) to ensure cohesion in the final piece.

3. HARMONY

Harmony refers to the pleasing arrangement of elements that creates a sense of unity within a design. This principle focuses on balance, coherence, and order, ensuring all components work together to form a visually satisfying whole. Achieving harmony involves deliberately using shapes, forms, colors, and textures to create consistency and connection.

When elements share similar characteristics or are thoughtfully organized to relate to one another, harmony emerges. Careful arrangement can produce a balanced and cohesive composition, even in asymmetrical designs. A harmonious design feels organized and unified, offering the viewer visual comfort and clarity.

Designers achieve harmony by strategically repeating shapes, colors, or patterns to establish visual consistency. This repetition is not about redundancy but rather a systematic approach to reinforcing unity. In a harmonious composition, every element contributes to the overall design, creating a sense of belonging without overwhelming the viewer.

Harmony is a cornerstone of both art and design for delivering a clear and cohesive message. It helps the audience engage with the work seamlessly, free from distractions caused by disjointed elements. True harmony is not merely about matching parts; crafting a visual flow that guides the viewer's eye effortlessly through the design. This balance fosters a sense of completeness and thoughtful craftsmanship.

At its essence, harmony serves as the underlying rhythm of design, blending diverse components into a unified narrative. It transcends mere aesthetics by imbuing each element with purpose and meaning. When achieved, harmony resonates intuitively, forging an emotional connection beyond the visual. Through careful attention to proportion, alignment, and spatial relationships, designers create instinctively correct layouts. This emotional resonance elevates harmony from a design principle to an art form, leaving a lasting impact by speaking to the viewer's heart and mind.

This image exemplifies harmony in design, where balanced arrangements of shapes, colors, and textures create a unified and visually pleasing space.

TASK

1. Exploring Harmony Through Composition
   - Create two separate compositions that demonstrate harmony:
     - Symmetrical Harmony: Use symmetrically arranged shapes, colors, and textures to create a balanced and unified design.
     - Asymmetrical Harmony: Achieve harmony through carefully arranging different elements that vary in size, shape, or color but still feel cohesive.
   - Reflect on how the arrangement of elements contributes to the overall sense of unity.

2. Harmony in Nature Observation
   - Observe and document examples of harmony in natural settings such as landscapes, flowers, or animal patterns.
   - Sketch or photograph these examples and describe how harmony is achieved through repetition, proportion, or alignment in the natural world.

3. Design Analysis
   - Select an artwork, graphic design, or architectural work that exemplifies harmony.
   - Analyze the elements contributing to the harmonious composition, such as color scheme, alignment, or balance.
   - Write a short reflection on how harmony enhances the viewer's experience of the work.

4. Creating Visual Flow
   - Design a layout (e.g., a poster, webpage, or magazine spread) that uses harmony to seamlessly guide the viewer's eye through the composition.
   - Experiment with alignment, spacing, and proportion to create an intuitive and engaging cohesive flow.

5. Collaborative Harmony Project (Optional)
   - Work with a group to create a mural or digital artwork that demonstrates harmony through the integration of diverse elements.
   - Assign roles to ensure each participant contributes different components while maintaining a unified overall design.

4. CONTRAST

Contrast is fundamentally about creating opposition. It emphasizes the juxtaposition of different elements to create visual interest and highlight differences. In design, contrast can be established through colors, shapes, textures, and even forms. For instance, placing a bright color against a dark background or using smooth versus rough textures can enhance a design's dynamism.

The term contrast refers to the relationship between two opposing elements. For instance, colors, shapes, and textures that are distinctly different from one another can be classified as having contrast. This principle is widely used in visual arts and design, and it is crucial in creating focal points and guiding viewers' attention.

In practice, contrast can be applied in numerous ways:

- Color Contrast involves using colors on opposite sides of the color wheel to create vivid and striking compositions. For example, red contrasts with green, yellow contrasts with purple, and blue contrasts with orange. These pairs are known as complementary colors.
- Shape Contrast: Involves using different shapes nearby, such as circles and squares, to generate visual interest.
- Size Contrast: Using objects of varying sizes within the same composition can create depth and focus, drawing attention to specific elements.
- Texture Contrast: Placing smooth textures against rough ones can emphasize surface differences, creating a tactile appeal.
- Directional Contrast: Utilizing opposing directions, such as horizontal versus vertical lines, can guide the eye and create movement within a piece.

By carefully implementing contrast, designers can ensure their compositions are not monotonous, thus maintaining the viewer's engagement.

This image highlights the power of contrast, where light and shadow interplay to create depth and direct attention within the composition.

This image captures the essence of contrast, showcasing the stark interplay between bold lines, shapes, and tonal variations to create visual intrigue and focus.

118

TASK

1. Exploring Color Contrast
   - Create a composition using complementary colors (e.g., red and green, blue and orange) to emphasize contrast.
   - Experiment with different intensities of the colors to observe their impact on visual interest and balance.
2. Shape and Size Contrast
   - Design a composition juxtaposing geometric and organic shapes to create visual interest.
   - Incorporate varying sizes of the shapes to highlight contrast and guide the viewer's attention effectively.
3. Texture Contrast Experiment
   - Create a collage or digital artwork that combines smooth and rough textures.
   - Reflect on how the tactile quality of textures influences the overall perception and dynamism of the composition.
4. Directional Contrast in Design
   - Design a poster that uses opposing directions (e.g., horizontal versus vertical lines) to create movement and dynamic tension.
   - Analyze how the use of directional contrast affects the flow and energy of the composition.
5. Real-Life Observation of Contrast
   - Capture or find three photographs that demonstrate different types of contrast (color, size, texture).
   - Write a short analysis of each image, describing how contrast enhances the visual appeal and focus within the context of the photograph.

In design, the best compositions are those where all the elements are harmoniously integrated. Unity ensures that all the elements are interconnected through balance. Each component of the design forms a coherent whole. In this sense, unity is achieved when elements that may seem contrasting or opposing are arranged to create a cohesive composition.

While it may seem paradoxical, opposite shapes can still contribute to a unified composition when they are organized within a structure of order and harmony. For instance, even elements with different forms, dimensions, or textures can be successfully integrated if they adhere to a shared rhythm or pattern.

Unity is one of the most fundamental principles in design. Whether it is a painting, a graphic design, or a piece of architecture, ensuring that all the parts work together as a cohesive unit is essential for achieving an aesthetically pleasing result. With unity, a composition can avoid appearing disjointed or chaotic.

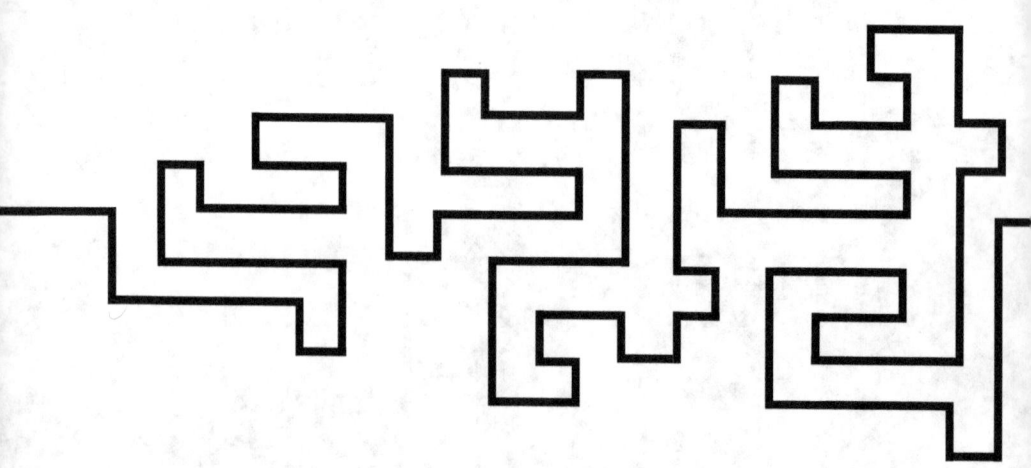

This image represents unity in design, where contrasting forms and patterns are harmonized to create a cohesive and balanced composition.

TASK

1. Creating Unified Compositions
   - Design a composition that integrates contrasting shapes, such as geometric and organic forms.
   - Arrange these elements within a balanced structure to achieve unity.
2. Exploring Rhythm and Pattern
   - Create a repetitive pattern using elements with varying textures or dimensions.
   - Analyze how the repetition contributes to the sense of unity in your design.
3. Opposites in Harmony
   - Develop a composition that combines large and small elements or light and dark tones.
   - Ensure the contrasting elements are arranged cohesively to avoid visual chaos.
4. Real-Life Observations of Unity
   - Find and document three examples of unity in real-world designs (e.g., architecture, product design, nature).
   - Write a short analysis of how the elements in each example work together to form a cohesive whole.
5. Collaborative Unity Project (Optional)
   - Work with a group to create a mural or digital artwork emphasizing unity.
   - Assign different tasks (e.g., color harmony, texture integration) to each participant to ensure all elements contribute to the final unified piece.

6. SPACING

Intervals are present everywhere in our lives. Nothing is continuous; there are always pauses, breaks, or spaces. In art, the principle of spacing is crucial in establishing a composition. Spacing allows a design to be perceived with a sense of rhythm and proportion. Using intervals significantly influences how the viewer perceives the work when creating art.

The spacing principle involves paying attention to the distances left between elements in a design. Small and closely packed intervals can create a monotonous and cramped feeling, whereas larger, irregular spaces can inject energy and dynamism into the composition, making it more visually compelling. Strategically using spacing in a design introduces a sense of depth and movement.

For example, in architectural layouts or designs with densely packed elements, a lack of spacing can make the arrangement feel rigid and uninviting. To avoid this effect, designers often incorporate spacing to break the monotony, creating a more balanced and engaging visual experience.

When designing, it's essential to find the right balance of spacing to enhance the aesthetic and functional aspects of the artwork. Elements arranged with thoughtful spacing create harmony and allow for a dynamic flow, enriching the overall impact of the design. This approach brings depth and excitement, transforming a composition from static to a piece that engages and captivates the observer.

This image exemplifies the principle of spacing, where deliberate intervals create a sense of balance, rhythm, and simplicity in the composition.

TASK

1. Exploring Spacing in Design
   - Create a series of compositions with varying intervals:
     - Use small, closely packed intervals in one composition.
     - Use larger, irregular intervals in another composition.
   - Compare the emotional and visual effects of each approach.
2. Spacing and Rhythm Experiment
   - Design a pattern emphasizing rhythm by alternating spacing between elements.
   - Analyze how variation in spacing affects the flow and movement of the composition.
3. Real-Life Spacing Observation
   - Identify three examples of effective spacing in real-life environments (e.g., urban planning, interior design, or nature).
   - Photograph or sketch each example and explain how spacing contributes to balance and engagement.
4. Dynamic Spacing Challenge
   - Create a digital or physical artwork incorporating dynamic spacing to guide the viewer's eye through the composition.
   - Use spacing intentionally to highlight focal points and create a sense of depth.
5. Collaborative Spacing Project (Optional)
   - Work in a group to create a large-scale mural or poster where spacing is used strategically.
   - Assign each participant a specific spacing approach (e.g., minimal, dynamic, or rhythmic) and combine the sections into a cohesive piece.

7. DOMINANCE - EMPHASIS

When constructing our designs, frequently using one of the visual arrangement elements within a composition can emphasize its significance, bringing it to the forefront and capturing our attention. By doing so, this element draws the observer's eye and becomes the focal point of the design.

In a composition, dominance can be established through various visual elements such as color, texture, line, shape, light, and shadow. If any of these elements take precedence, it becomes the dominant feature, naturally attracting the viewer's attention.

Dominance can also be expressed in terms of form. For instance, the shapes that stand out in a composition communicate a lot about the language of the design while also imparting a sense of dynamism. Unity, dominance, and repetition together create harmony. The repetition of forms reflects the simplicity and regularity of natural order, a fundamental principle in design.

Certain forms must be emphasized in compositions to ensure the design remains engaging while achieving balance. This balance is visual and functional, adding interest to the design while maintaining harmony.

For example, if we establish dominance through color, we must carefully select the color group that will stand out. While warm colors dominate naturally, cool colors require a controlled approach to achieve emphasis. In such cases, the dominant color used within the work will shape the overall emotional impression conveyed to the observer.

By carefully controlling dominance, a designer can guide the viewer's experience, ensuring the composition delivers visual impact and clear communication of its intended message.

This image illustrates dominance, where the raised hand emerges as the focal point, guiding the viewer's attention amidst the tranquil setting.

TASK

1. Exploring Dominance in Design
   - Create three compositions, each emphasizing dominance through a different visual element:
     - Use color dominance in one composition by highlighting a specific color group.
     - Establish texture dominance in another composition, contrasting smooth and rough surfaces.
     - Emphasize form dominance in the third composition by using bold, standout shapes.
2. Dominance and Emotion
   - Design a piece that conveys a specific emotion using dominance.
   - Write a short explanation of how the chosen dominant element (e.g., color, texture, or form) contributes to the intended emotional tone.
3. Real-Life Examples of Dominance
   - Find and photograph three examples of dominance in everyday environments (e.g., advertising, architecture, or nature).
   - Analyze each example:
     - Explain how dominance is established.
     - Discuss its impact on the observer and how it guides focus.
4. Dynamic Dominance Challenge
   - Create a composition that combines dominance with balance and repetition.
   - Use your chosen dominant element to guide the viewer's attention while ensuring the composition remains harmonious and engaging.
5. Collaborative Dominance Project (Optional)
   - Work with a group to create a mural or poster that explores dominance through multiple visual elements.
   - Assign each participant an element to dominate (e.g., color, shape, or texture) and ensure all sections integrate cohesively into a unified design.

8. SCALE AND PROPORTION

In design, the principle of scale and proportion involves using objects of varying sizes about each other to establish a harmonious balance. The relationship between scale, proportion, and the elements within a design is crucial. Achieving this harmony ensures that compositions maintain visual and structural balance, which is essential for functional and artistic effectiveness.

The concept of proportion in art is often associated with measurements and ratios. These ratios can significantly affect how a piece is perceived, whether it's a painting, sculpture, or any other visual composition. Accurate scaling in a design can influence how a viewer perceives depth, space, and importance within the composition.

When examining a piece of artwork, we are often drawn to how accurately proportion and scale have been used. A successful design uses these principles to guide the viewer's eye, create focus, and convey the intended message effectively. Proper proportion not only ensures balance but also enhances the aesthetic appeal of a piece.

For example, in a visual artwork, the harmonious arrangement of different elements in proportion can produce a cohesive and striking effect. On the other hand, misuse or distortion of scale can disrupt the visual flow, making the composition feel disjointed or off-balance.

We are constantly surrounded by varying scales and proportions, from architecture to interior design. The relationship between objects, whether furniture in a room or the elements of a painting, influences how we perceive and interact with our environment.

Understanding and mastering scale and proportion are fundamental skills for any designer or artist, as they directly impact the success of a visual composition.

This image demonstrates the principle of scale and proportion, where the balance between the two planters creates harmony and visual interest within the composition.

TASK

1. Exploring Scale and Proportion in Art
   - Create three compositions demonstrating different uses of scale and proportion:
     - Exaggerated Proportions: Design a surreal or dramatic composition using distorted proportions.
     - Realistic Proportions: Develop a piece with accurate, realistic proportions to achieve harmony.
     - Contrasting Scales: Experiment with varying scales in a single composition to highlight depth or hierarchy.
2. Proportion Ratios in Design
   - Use the golden ratio or another proportional system to create a balanced composition.
   - Write a brief explanation of how the chosen ratio affects your design's harmony and visual appeal.
3. Real-Life Observation
   - Capture photographs or create sketches of scale and proportion examples in everyday settings (e.g., architecture, furniture, or nature).
   - Analyze these examples:
     - Discuss how scale and proportion contribute to their balance and functionality.
4. Scale and Emotion
   - Design a piece where scale is deliberately used to evoke a specific emotion:
     - Small elements can create intimacy or delicacy.
     - Large elements can evoke grandeur or awe.
   - Include a short paragraph explaining your design choices and emotional intent.
5. Collaborative Proportion Project (Optional)
   - Collaborate with a group to create a mural or 3D installation that explores varying scales and proportions.
   - Assign specific proportions or scales to each participant, ensuring the final composition is cohesive and visually engaging.

07
THREE-DIMENSIONAL DESIGNS

Three-dimensional works have been utilized throughout history, producing significant pieces spanning various art disciplines. Beyond its historical roots, three-dimensional applications are extensively used in fields like architecture, providing depth and form to structures. These techniques aim to teach learners an understanding of depth, shapes, and spatial relationships.

In three-dimensional design, the focus is on teaching how to perceive and interpret height, depth, and width as a cohesive whole. Such exercises envelop objects within boundaries, emphasizing both interior and exterior space. These projects can involve natural and artificial materials, including paper, cardboard, clay, wood, metal, and synthetic substances. Different materials can be employed individually or combined to create complex three-dimensional structures.

The materials can also be repurposed to create new objects or reconstructed into original forms. Creating with these materials involves integrating selected elements into a system that embodies order and harmony. The key elements to consider in three-dimensional modeling include shape, tone, space, texture, line, color, and even the dimension of time.

Understanding and mastering these principles allows a designer to transform basic materials into expressive works that convey depth, volume, and a sense of place within a composition.

This image highlights the principles of three-dimensional design, blending form, depth, and material to create a harmonious spatial composition.

08
CONCLUSION

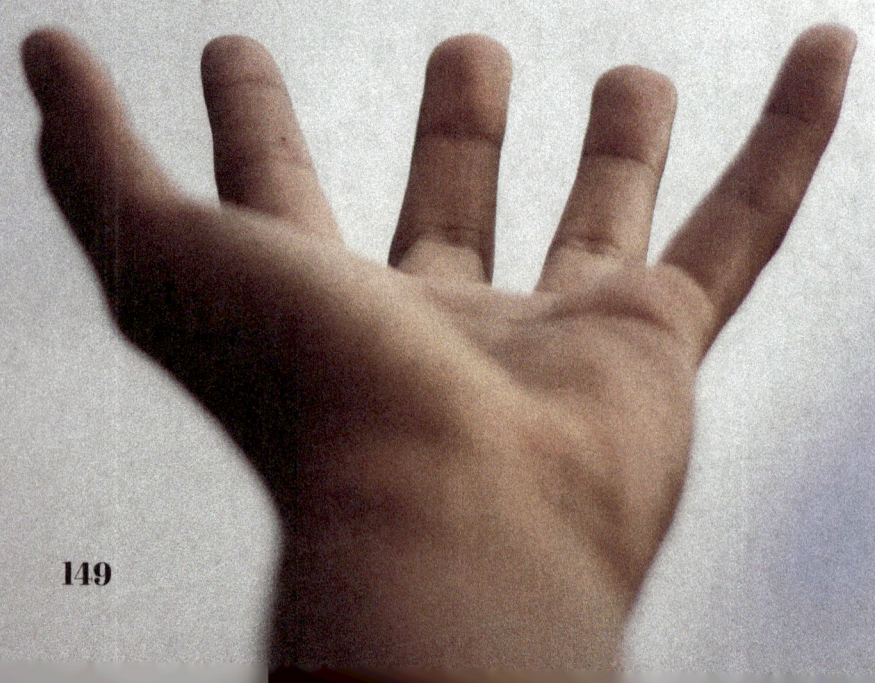

In the context of design education, one of the primary objectives is to prepare students for their future professional lives, instilling in them the foundational elements and principles of art and design. The focus of this process is to convey the knowledge of how to approach the creative process and effectively apply materials in diverse design contexts. By doing so, the educational journey enables the student to gain proficiency in handling materials, experimenting with different techniques, and understanding their applications within a creative framework.

The growth and development achieved through this process encourage learners to expand their horizons, exploring connections between various materials, themes, and principles. Workshops dedicated to fundamental design are structured to immerse students in the world of materials, empowering them to recognize, select, and utilize these resources efficiently in their projects. This hands-on approach equips students with the foundational skills necessary for further education. By the end of their journey, learners will have developed the ability to apply their skills in real-world scenarios, enhancing their creative problem-solving abilities.

In the rapidly evolving landscape of technology, it has become imperative for design education to keep pace with advancements. The design course offered during the first year of university aims to equip students with an understanding of art's essential principles and elements, encouraging them to think critically and creatively. Integrating digital tools in the design process complements traditional methods and enhances the teaching and learning experience, making it more engaging and relevant.

Given today's technological advancements, there is a clear need for integrating design programs with computer-based systems. This ensures that the foundational principles are taught comprehensively and applied consistently throughout the curriculum. By incorporating up-to-date software support, students are better equipped to adapt to the evolving demands of the industry. Thus, by leveraging the support provided by technology, the course transforms into a more dynamic and effective learning environment, preparing students for the challenges of the future.

REFERENCES

- A Project By A Laurentian Architecture Graduate Is Recognized. https://www.commercialarchitecturemagazine.com/a-project-by-a-laurentian-architecture-graduate/

- Bauhaus Unmasked: Unveiling Nazi Links to Design Icons.. https://shuttech.com/design/architecture/exposing-bauhaus-betrayal-revealing-nazi-ties-and-shadows-on-design-icons-legacies-in-shocking-investigation/.

- The Bauhaus Movement: Shaping Modern Art & Design – LelloLiving. https://lelloliving.com/en-us/blogs/blog/the-bauhaus-movement-shaping-modern-art-and-design

- Ozenen, G. (2023). Terms Used in Lighting. https://doi.org/10.1007/978-3-031-49695-0_1

- What Is the Use of Color Theory in Graphic Design – Exploring the Power of Graphic Design with Grafiscopio.com. https://www.grafiscopio.com/what-is-the-use-of-color-theory-in-graphic-design/

- Cicekli, U. (2003). Computational model for heat transfer in the human eye using the finite element method. https://core.ac.uk/download/217400135.pdf

- Color Psychology: Enhancing Your Space with the Right Hues – Interior Design. https://blockspare.com/demo/default/interior-design/2023/08/15/color-psychology-enhancing-your-space-with-the-right-hues/

- The Artistry of Color Palettes: Unlocking Visual Harmony and Captivating Designs - archivo. Design. https://archivo.design/uncategorized/color-palettes/

- 10+ Best Youtube Thumbnails With Examples In 2024 - TubeLoop. https://tubeloop.io/best-youtube-thumbnails/

- Best Teal Color Guide (With Hex Codes & Color Swatches. https://www.notebookandpenguin.com/teal-color/

www.ingramcontent.com/pod-product-compliance
Lightning Source LLC
Chambersburg PA
CBHW071028240526
45469CB00006BD/2136